'Know the Game' Series

SHOW JUMPING

CONTENTS

Foreword

TODAY Show Jumping is regarded as one of the leading National sports of this country. It not only requires a high standard of training but it also entails great courage from both horse and rider. This sport provides an enthralling and exciting spectacle.

Perhaps one of the leading factors in bringing about its great popularity is the simplicity of the rules, as a spectator with little knowledge can soon learn to judge for himself. It is one of the few, if not the only sport, in which there are no doubtful decisions.

However, riders and spectators will certainly derive greater pleasure if they understand the technique. More enjoyment will be gained by the spectator who has studied the finer points, the building of the obstacles, the layout of the course, the methods used by the riders to overcome the variety of problems, and the rules.

In recent years our riders have raised Britain's prestige, and I hope this book will help some, who join these riders, and at the same time also help those many spectators, who cheer them on to victory, to derive even greater interest. Surely the greater the knowledge, the greater the interest, and this book certainly provides the opportunity to gain that knowledge.

M. P. Ansell.

Colonel Sir Michael Ansell, C.B.E., D.S.O., D.L.,
President, British Equestrian Federation

THE BRITISH SHOW JUMPING ASSOCIATION

This is the parent body of Show Jumping in England which has been responsible for our great victories at the Olympic Games since the war, at all the main shows in Europe, and also in Canada and America.

Even if you do not own a show-jumper yourself, join the Association and help our Team to victory at the next Olympic Games. As a non-jumping member you get a badge and details of the 1,000 shows which are affiliated to the Association. If you own a pony or a horse you can insure it under the exceptionally good and inexpensive scheme to which your membership entitles you.

The current annual rates of subscription are:

Junior Members	£1.50
Associate Members	£2.00
Non-Jumping Members	£2.00
Jumping Members	£5.00

For full particulars apply to:
THE SECRETARY-GENERAL
THE BRITISH SHOW JUMPING ASSOCIATION
NATIONAL EQUESTRIAN CENTRE,
KENILWORTH WARWICKSHIRE. CV8 2LR

The History of Show Jumping

For many centuries the horse has been the friend and servant of man. This noble animal has helped to win wars, has for many years been the most important form of transport, and has been a companion in sport whether it be riding, driving, hunting or racing.

In the early days, whether in battle or in sport, it was not necessary that the horse should jump, except perhaps a ditch or small bank; however in the eight-eenth century, with the passing of the Enclosure Act, the situation changed. No longer was it possible to cross the country without jumping, and the rider soon realised not only how well the horse could jump, but also the thrill of this new form of horsemanship.

The birth of Show Jumping took place in 1866 when a class for show jumpers was arranged at a Harness Show in Paris. The horse and rider first appeared in the ring to parade before the public and were then sent out into the nearby country to jump some natural obstacles. This was of little interest to the spectator and, soon after, it was so organised that a few simple fences were built in the arena. Fifteen years later the sport came to England, to be known as "Lepping" competitions. By 1900, "lepping" or jumping competitions took place at the more important shows, but entries were small, seldom exceeding fifteen or twenty, and ladies riding side-saddle competed in special classes.

In 1912 Jumping was first included among the Equestrian events of the Olympic Games, but each country had its own rules, and so the Federation Equestre Internationale came into being, to standardise these. In Britain there were no standard rules, and each Show decided how the judging should be conducted, and many of the marks were given for style. This led to dissatisfaction and confusion to the spectator, and the British Show Jumping Association was formed to standardise the judging of Jumping Competitions.

The first International Horse Show in England took place at Olympia in 1907, and in course of time this Show has become the scene of the finest jumping competitions in England. At the first Show, the most important competition was for teams of officers representing their country, who competed for the King Edward VII Challenge Cup, which was won outright by the Russian Team in 1914. When the Show restarted after the 1914-1918 war a new perpetual Challenge Cup was presented by Edward, Prince of Wales, and this today is the major Team competition at the Show. In 1910 King George V presented a Challenge Cup for individual competition, which was won outright by Captain J. A. Talbot-Ponsonby in 1934. The trophy was re-presented, and today remains the coveted individual prize of the Show Jumping world.

Show Jumping has thrived throughout the country, particularly since the last war, and has now become a national sport. In the early part of this century few people visited horse shows apart from connoisseurs of the horse. Today, the picture has changed and this sport has a great following, which is shown by the attendance records being broken each year at the Royal International Horse Show, where some 60,000 spectators attend annually.

During the summer the B.S.J.A. have approx. 1,000 Shows under their jurisdiction, and many hundreds of thousands flock to the ringside to watch the jumping classes.

Today there are over ten thousand horses and ponies competing throughout the country, a figure which incidentally even exceeds the number of race horses in training. The British International Jumping Teams have more than proved themselves, with endless victories throughout the world.

Administration of Show Jumping

International Show Jumping is controlled throughout the world by the "FEDERATION EQUESTRE INTERNATIONALE" (F.E.I.) which also controls the equestrian events of the Olympic Games.

The F.E.I. is an international equestrian union of the National Federations of some forty countries each of which agrees to comply with the statutes and general regulations of the F.E.I.

The Committee of the F.E.I. is made up of two representatives of each affiliated nation and meets once a year. This committee elects, by secret vote, from amongst its members, a bureau of eight members who serve for four years and might be termed the "Board of Directors". Great Britain is at present represented on the Bureau of the F.E.I.

The National Federation of Great Britain is the British Equestrian Federation, National Equestrian Centre, Kenilworth, Warwickshire, CV8 2LR, and the B.S.J.A. has equal representation on this Federation with the British Horse Society.

The B.S.J.A. is, therefore, the controlling body of Show Jumping in Great Britain, and is responsible for framing the National Rules. Every show of repute that includes Show Jumping Classes in its schedule is now affiliated to the B.S.J.A. and holds its competitions under rules and regulations approved by this Association.

The Competition

If the horse jumps clear, style does not count but—

A jumping competition is one in which horse and rider are tested under various conditions over a course of obstacles. It is a test of the horse's jumping capabilities. If the competitor makes certain defined mistakes; knocking down the jumps, refusing, etc., he is penalised or faulted. The winner of the competition is the competitor who incurs the least number of faults. The style of the horse or the rider has no influence on the result, provided that no faults are incurred. However, it is certain that the better trained horse, with a good rider, will have an advantage over the horse with perhaps the same capabilities, which has not been so well trained and is badly ridden.

All Jumping Competitions at National Horse Shows are judged under B.S.J.A. Rules and Regulations. The competitions are varied so that competitors may select the most suitable for their horse and the spectator may be offered greater and more varied entertainment. These competitions are divided into six main categories:

—the better-trained horse well-ridden will have the advantage

(i) those in which, if competitors are still equal after two jumps-off, the prize money is divided. These are judged under Table "A1".

(ii) those in which competitors jump against the clock in the second jump-off, the competitor with the least number of faults in the fastest time being the winner. These are judged under Table "A2".

(iii) Those in which competitors jump against the clock in the first jump-off, the competitor with the ieast number of faults in the fastest time being the winner. These are judged under Table "A3".

(iv) those in which competitors jump against the clock in the first round of the competition, so that the competitor with the least number of faults in the fastest time is the winner. These are judged under Table "A4".

(v) those in which 6-10 seconds are added to the total time taken by the competitor, for each obstacle knocked down, and the winner is the competitor with the shortest total time. These include the Take Your Own Line, Scurry and Pair Relay competition, and are judged under Table "S" (Speed).

(vi) certain competitions, such as Hit and Hurry, Accumulator, Have-a-Gamble and Gamblers have their own special rules for judging. The details of these are given later.

At all International Horse Shows, the competitions are judged under International or F.E.I. Rules, which are almost identical with the B.S.J.A. rules outlined above.

1 2 3

Horse and Rider when Jumping

Whether it be conducting an orchestra or playing cricket there are orthodox and unorthodox methods and styles. The orthodox, or what might be termed the correct style, will usually meet with the greater success, but it would be a mistake to suggest that other styles were wrong. In riding, as in many a sport, the greatest artist has a technique of his own, and if it attains success it would be unfair to offer criticism.

The jump may be divided into four stages, the Approach, the Take-off, the Jump and the Landing, and the rider should, when jumping, base his methods on the following principles. During each phase he will suit his style to the movements of the horse, and throughout he must be in complete harmony with his horse.

The approach (Fig. 1)

During the approach the horse will be balancing himself by placing his head and neck down and forward; the rider will be sitting still, and slightly forward, his hands maintaining a contact with the horse by means of the reins. The rider's legs will be pressed against the horse's sides urging him forward.

The take-off

When the horse is taking off he does so in two stages.

First he pushes his forehand upwards by driving off his front legs, during which time the hindlegs are brought underneath the body (Fig. 2). The hindquarters and hocks then propel the body upwards and forwards over the top of the obstacle (Fig. 3).

The rider must, during the approach and take-off, sit slightly forward, remaining still so that he does not interfere with the movement of the horse, and must always be perfectly balanced.

The jump (Figs. 4 and 5)

During the actual jump the horse will stretch his head forward and down whilst in mid-air. He uses his head and neck to maintain his balance, and by bringing the weight forward makes it easier to lift the hindquarters over the jump. The rider, throughout the jump, must follow these movements of the horse, and this will necessitate his being forward in the saddle. The horse will raise the head and neck as the hindquarters come down and his forehand lands.

The landing (Fig. 6)

As the horse lands, his head, having come slightly up, now stretches out and is lowered again in order to enable him to go forward. The rider must again remain balanced and should once more be slightly forward.

The Course and the Obstacles

Since a jumping competition is decided on the way the horse jumps the fences, the chief consideration must always be the layout of the course and the building of the obstacles. It must always be remembered that the intention of the builder is to promote good natural jumping. Although the fences may be big they should encourage the horse and rider to meet them with confidence.

Neither the Federation Equestre Internationale, nor the British Show Jumping Association wish to regularise courses or obstacles, and recognise that greater variety creates a precious element of interest, which should at all costs be encouraged. Thus there is no set type of course or obstacle, and the more important shows each have their own characteristics.

Generally the course will vary from 457-823m (500-900 yds.), and in this will be included ten to sixteen fences. Fences should be strong and heavy in appearance; as far as possible they should be built to resemble natural hazards of the countryside. This at times will be difficult, as fences should be bright and cheerful in order that they may be pleasing both to the spectator and the rider. Further it must be remembered that the fence must be so coloured that it will stand out in any light against a background of innumerable faces, coloured dresses, and motor cars around the side of the arena.

There are certain definite terms used when discussing obstacles, and the main are as follows:

THE TRACK

The track is the path which must be followed by the rider to complete any course. The distance of the course is measured along this track and must be correct to a few metres.

THE FENCES

Each fence requires the horse to make one single jump or effort. (Banks excepted.) Faults are always recorded at each fence.

Fences will be varied, but in the main they may be divided into two categories:

The straight fence

The straight fence is one so built that all the elements of which it is composed are placed vertical to the ground, and one above each other in the same plane.

The more common straight fences are: Gates; Walls; Post and Rails; Single Rail.

These are varied by their construction and colouring. The heights will vary, but a white gate of 1.45m (4 ft. 9 ins.) or more is indeed a formidable obstacle. The wall at 1.40m (4 ft. 6 ins.), if well built, should provide little difficulty, and in Championship Classes it will be jumped at 1.70m (5 ft. 6 ins.) or more. A single rail at 1.30m (4 ft. 3 ins.) may be difficult, but if more rails are added below it, it will become a simple test.

Narrow fences, such as the stile, the small wicket gate or short poles placed in a gap, are a test of the obedience of the horse.

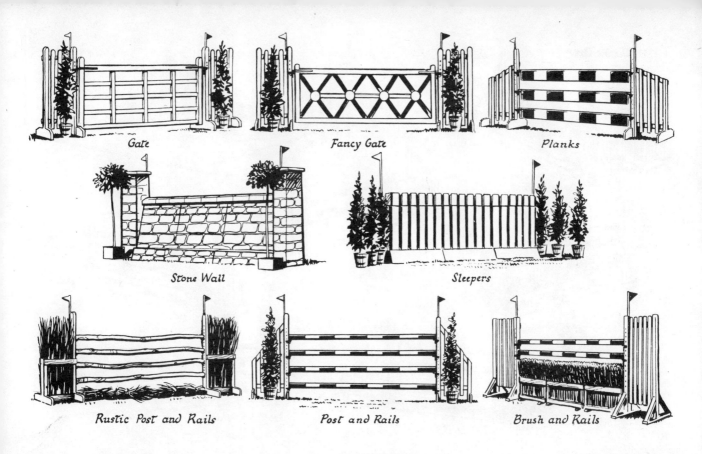

Gate

Fancy Gate

Planks

Stone Wall

Sleepers

Rustic Post and Rails

Post and Rails

Brush and Rails

Typical "straight" fences

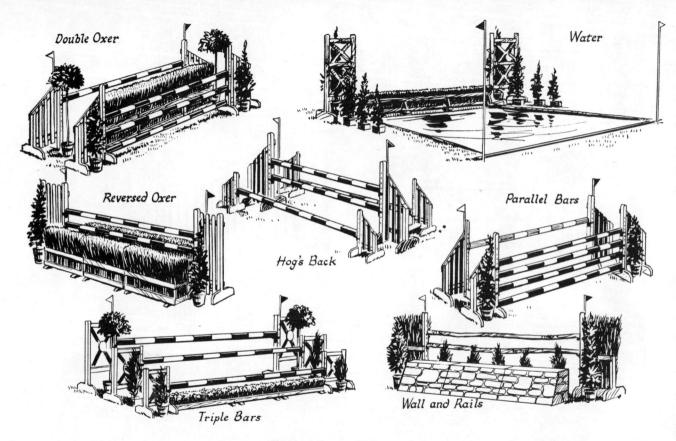

Double Oxer

Water

Reversed Oxer

Parallel Bars

Hog's Back

Triple Bars

Wall and Rails

Typical "spread" fences

The spread fence

The spread fence is so built that it necessitates the horse jumping width, as well as height.

Among the "spread" fences the most usual are: Triple Bars; Double-oxer; Hog's Back; Parallel Bars; Water.

Rails may also be added to the wall or other common straight fences making them into spreads. As in the case of straight fences, the heights and spreads will vary considerably. A triple bar of 1.45m (4 ft. 9 ins.) with a spread of 1.80-2m (6 or 7 ft.) will easily be jumped by a good horse, whereas parallel bars standing at 1.40m (4 ft. 6 ins.) with a spread of 1.80m (6 ft.) will present a severe problem.

The water will vary between 3.65m and 4.90m (12 ft. and 16 ft.) overall, with a small hedge on the take-off side about 60cm (2 ft.) high, sloping towards the water.

THE GROUND LINE

When approaching a fence, the horse judges the point at which he intends to take off by looking at the line at the base of the fence, which is called the Ground Line.

In order to jump with success, a horse must take off at the correct spot. A fence, such as the wall, which rests on the ground, has a distinct ground line. A single rail has no ground line, and this makes it a difficult fence.

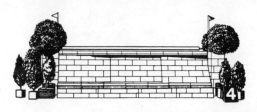

A fence such as the wall has a distinct ground line

A horse is inclined to take off from a point too close to the fence, and therefore it will be made easier if the ground line is slightly on the approach side of the fence. If, on the other hand, the fence is composed of a single rail about 90cm (3 ft.) high, placed on the take-off side of a brush, wall, or hedge, the horse will be judging his distance from the base of the brush, wall, or hedge, thereby getting too close to the rail. This is known as a False Ground Line.

In Novice Competitions the Ground Line must be clearly defined. A loose pole on the ground must be pegged down.

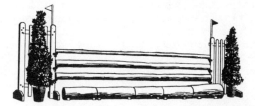

This fence is made easier since the ground line is slightly on the approach side of the fence

False ground line (see previous page)

COURSE BUILDING

Each fence should provide a definite problem to the rider. It should always be made as wide as possible, i.e. from wingstand to wingstand; the greater the height the greater the width; as a guide, fences should not be less than 3.35m (11 ft.) wide. Care must always be taken that the obstacle is free, and that if hit hard no part of it will become entangled with the uprights or wings. Certain main components are common to practically every fence. They are: Stands; Poles; Wings; Cups in which the poles rest, and Flags.

In addition, brush fences, gates and a variety of walls are used. With the help of these and poles almost any fence may be built.

The wings are to show clearly to the horse the extremities of the fence. They should be carefully placed slightly in front of the fence, to encourage the horse towards the centre of the fence. All gaps must be blocked out with pillars or shrubs.

The poles are used to represent the rails of the natural fence. They are usually held in cups and should not fall unless hit hard. The poles should be solid and about 11.25cm (4½ ins.) in diameter. They are usually made of ash, larch or pine, and a 3.65m (12 ft.) pole will weigh between 18 kg and 23 kg.

The cup in which the pole rests is made of steel or cast iron, and has sufficient depth to hold the pole when touched or tapped. As a guide, the cup should be of sufficient depth to allow one third of the pole to rest within it.

The wings are to show clearly the extremity of the fence.
All gaps must be blocked out with pillars or shrubs

THE HEIGHTS OF THE FENCES

It is quite impossible to give any set measurements for fences as these depend upon a variety of circumstances governed by the conditions of the competition.

However, there are certain principles applicable to all courses.

(i) Whatever the competition, at its conclusion at least one competitor should have jumped the course without fault, as otherwise it can truly be said that the course was too severe.

(ii) The faults should be found to be distributed evenly between all the fences with the exception of the first two or three.

(iii) The first fence, and the second, should be simple, as the horses must be encouraged to jump with confidence.

(iv) In competitions which are designed for speed, the fences should never be high. These competitions are a test of jumping obedience at speed and with the additional assistance of time, a result is always obtained after one round. (Such competitions are: "Fault and Out", "Relay", "Take Your Own Line" and "Hunting" ("Scurry").

The International Rules only lay down conditions for heights in the Nation's Cup Competitions.

The B.S.J.A. do not lay down any general conditions as to heights of fences, except for the maximum heights in certain competitions

When the "going" is bad, the heights will be less

A well-made fence can be built larger than—

—a flimsy fence which suggests to the horse that it is easier to knock down than to jump

There are certain factors which must always be taken into account when considering the heights of the fences.

(i) The condition of the ground.

(ii) The position of the fence in the course; if placed early it should be smaller than if it is to be met when the horse and rider have got into their stride.

(iii) The setting of the fence; if it is placed immediately after a sharp turn, with only a short approach, or the background makes the obstacle difficult to see, the fence should be small.

(iv) The nature of the fence, and the material with which it is made; a well made fence, solid in appearance, and attractive to jump, can be built larger than a flimsy one which suggests to the horse that it is easier to knock it down than to jump it.

To sum up, the Clerk of the Course will consider first the conditions of the competition, secondly the standard of the competitors, and lastly the quality of the obstacles and the state of the ground.

WORLD JUMPING RECORDS

The following are recognised by the F.E.I. as being the present record:

High Jump

Captain A. Larraguibel at Santiago, Chile, riding "Huaso" on 5th February, 1949, cleared 2.47m (8 ft. 0¼ ins.).

Long Jump

Colonel Lopez Del Hierro of Spain, riding "Amado Mio" in 1951 cleared 8.30m (27 ft. 2 ins.).

A treble

COMBINATIONS OF FENCES

If two or more fences are placed so that they follow directly one after the other, and if the inside distance between any two does not exceed 12m (39 ft. 4 ins.), whether there are two or more fences, they will be regarded as a combination and, except in special cases, will be numbered as one obstacle.

Combinations should be included in all courses as these obstacles test the suppleness and obedience of the horse, and not only provide variety but a good spectacle.

The distance between the fences is varied. It may be arranged so that it is easy for either one or two non-jumping strides of the horse. On the other hand it may be difficult and the rider must then decide how he will deal with the problem; he will either have to shorten or lengthen the stride of his horse by checking, decreasing or increasing his speed.

The distance between the fences will depend on two main factors:
  (i) The number of non-jumping strides it is intended that the horse should take.
  (ii) The height and nature of the fences and how they are placed.

When referring to a non-jumping stride it means

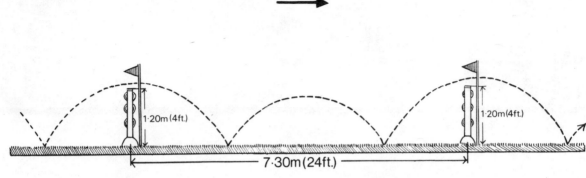

The easy distance for one non-jumping stride is 7.30m - 8m (24 ft - 26 ft.)

the stride taken by the horse after landing and before taking off at the next fence. The stride of the horse will vary according to its size and way of galloping. The average stride at the gallop may be taken as 3m (10 ft.). Should the horse be going slowly it may be less, whereas if "galloping on" it may be more.

The height and nature of the fence will decide where the horse will take off and land. When jumping a small fence the horse will not land as far away as if jumping a higher fence, and should the fence be a "spread" he will land further over as he will be going at a faster pace in order to jump the distance.

Between two "straight" fences 1.20m (4 ft.) high, the easy distance for a horse to take one non-jumping stride is 7.30m (24 ft.). The distance for two non-jumping strides is 10m-10.65m (33 ft.-36 ft.). If it is required that these distances remain easy with larger fences, they must be increased.

These distances will be varied on occasions. If the combination is composed of a "spread" fence, followed by a "straight" fence, the distance will be increased to remain easy. The horse will have to approach the first, a "spread", at a fast speed, and will therefore land further out into the double. On the other hand, if the first is a "straight" and the second a

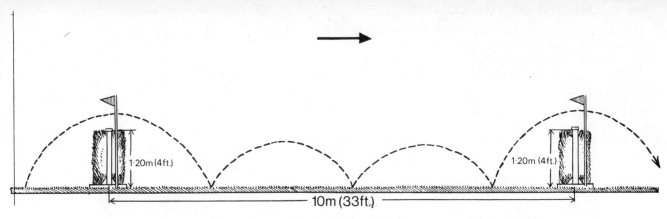

The easy distance for two non-jumping strides is 10m - 11m (33 ft. - 36 ft.)

"spread", the distance will be reduced, otherwise the horse will have to "reach" for the second fence.

If the competition requires that the horse should jump at speed the distances may be increased, and vice versa.

Combinations may consist of any type of fence, and when two or more are included in a course, they should vary both in distance and arrangement. On one occasion the "straight" fence will be placed before the "spread", on another the "spread" will be first. It should however be remembered that, when the "straight" follows the "spread", it is a more severe test because the horse, having been extended, must be collected in a short distance.

Distances should at times be made difficult for the stride as this will necessitate the rider thinking carefully how he will approach the fences. The distance between fences is always of interest and the builder of the course will watch the first few horses with excitement, wondering whether his measurements are correct for the test he has set. From outside the ring, the experienced rider, whose turn is yet to come, will watch the other competitors so that he can decide the best way of jumping.

THE PLANNING OF THE COURSE

It is difficult to specify a standard size of an arena, but one of approximately 73m (80 yds.) wide and 110m (120 yds.) long is excellent.

The planning of a good course requires much time but the builder will derive pleasure and pride from his finished production. The provision of well-made fences and carefully planned courses will always produce jumping of a high standard, which will give pleasure to the competitor and the spectator.

The following principles should be observed:

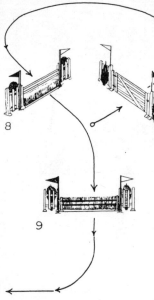

The course should always include at least one change of direction

(i) As many fences as possible should be used; an ordinary course should have at least nine or ten obstacles even should this necessitate jumping some twice.

(ii) The course should always necessitate at least one change of direction, if possible two or three.

(iii) "Straight" and "spread" fences should be alternated where practicable.

(iv) There should be at least one combination, two if possible.

(v) The simple fences should be placed early in the course so that horse and rider are given confidence as they warm up.

(vi) The maximum length of any course will be governed by the number of obstacles included in it with a maximum of 65⅔ yards or 60 metres per obstacle.

(vii) The minimum length of a course under F.E.I. rules, Table B, will be 763 yards or 700 metres long.

The stile jump to test him in obedience

Every fence should be placed with a particular test in mind: the combination to test the horse for obedience and suppleness; the stile jump to test him in obedience when approaching the narrow fence; and the high wall to test his ability to jump great heights.

The distances between obstacles should vary. As a general rule they should not be less than 15m (49 ft.) and obviously a longer approach will be required before a large "spread".

The course having been carefully built, the Clerk

The high wall as a test of the horse's ability to jump great heights

of the Course checks each fence. He notes the position of each part of the fence in case it is knocked down. He checks the position of the flags and numbers.

Measuring the course with a wheel

MEASURING THE COURSE

Every course is measured. This is done either with a measuring wheel or by pacing the actual track which would be followed by a careful rider not wishing to take chances by cutting corners.

THE PLAN OF THE COURSE

A plan of the course is displayed on a board in the collecting ring at least one hour before the commencement of the competition.

The plan shows clearly the direction in which the fences are to be jumped. Each fence is numbered but the nature of the fence is not indicated. Any special conditions of the competition are stated on the plan and include the details of the jump-off if there is to be one.

The Distance, Time Allowed, and Time Limit must all be shown on the plan. For a competition under Tables B. or C. the time penalty must be shown.

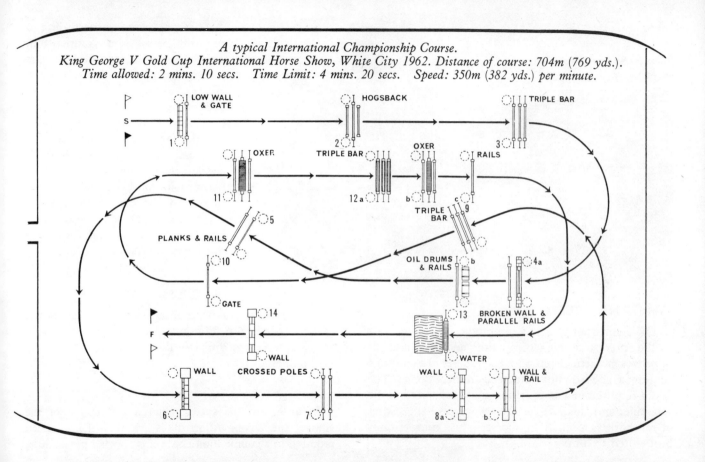

A typical International Championship Course.
King George V Gold Cup International Horse Show, White City 1962. Distance of course: 704m (769 yds.).
Time allowed: 2 mins. 10 secs.   Time Limit: 4 mins. 20 secs.   Speed: 350m (382 yds.) per minute.

The speed will vary according to the objects of the competition. There are competitions for the horse that, ridden slowly, has the greatest ability to jump heights, and there are competitions which provide a test of obedience at speed in addition to jumping. In the first case, although there will be an element of time, it will be slow because jumping is the first consideration. In the second case, a combination of obedience and jumping is required and, therefore, the speed will be faster.

TIME AND SPEED

The element of time in a jumping competition adds to the interest of both competitor and spectator. It improves horsemanship and encourages the rider to acquire a good-quality and well-trained horse. The speed required in a competition is always stated in the schedule, and this enables the owner, like the owner of racehorses, to enter his horse in the competitions best suited to him.

Both National and International Rules lay down certain speeds for different competitions and these are decided according to the type and objects of the competition.

According to the speed required and length of the course, the "Time Allowed" is set, thus if the speed required in a competition is 275m (300 yds.) per minute, and the length of the course is 275m (300 yds.), the "Time Allowed" would be 1 minute. The Time Limit in all jumping competitions is twice the "Time Allowed" and therefore in this case would be 2 minutes.

The "Time" of the competitor is the time he takes in riding the course from the moment he crosses the starting line until he crosses the finishing line mounted. In special circumstances time is taken off and these circumstances are clearly stated in the Rules. The "Time" is recorded in seconds and fifths of a second, either by automatic or hand methods. The most common method is for the competitor to break a ray at the start which completes a circuit starting a clock in the Judges' Box, and on crossing the finishing line a second ray or thread is broken which breaks the circuit and stops the clock. Accurate timing can be done by hand, provided the official is continuously alert.

In conclusion, the element of "Time" adds considerably to the interest of spectators, and surely the horse that can jump his fences with precision at speed, deserves the credit. Further, the "Time" element not only adds variety to the programme, but it gives the chance of success to more than one type of horse.

WALKING THE COURSE

The rider must always be permitted to walk the course, dismounted, at a time prior to the commencement of a Competition, but once the Competition has started no further inspection will be permitted, even before a jump-off. The rider should never miss this opportunity of preparing himself for the competition because this is just as important as the actual ride.

As time is often short, competitors should realise that this is not the occasion to meet friends and have a pleasant chat in the arena. It is the chance to study the course over which they will shortly compete.

Having studied the plan of the course, and the conditions, the competitor should walk it conscientiously from beginning to end along the exact track on which he intends to ride.

He should study each fence, consider its nature, and how he will jump it. Combinations must receive particular attention and the distances between the fences should be examined because these will decide the speed of the approach.

The rider should plan in advance the turns he should make; throughout the round the course should come to him as second nature.

The solidity of the obstacles is important; the rider must examine them carefully to ascertain at which jump he can ride with less care, and if necessary take risks. At the same time he will decide where he can ride for time if this is necessary, and at which fences he must take no chances and must approach straight. Should he decide to make time he may have to cut corners, and this possibility will mean taking fences at

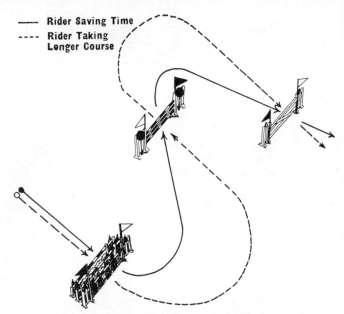

—— Rider Saving Time
---- Rider Taking Longer Course

In order to make time the rider may decide to cut corners

an angle. If the fence is straight this should not present any great difficulty to a horse, but, if the fence is a spread it must be remembered that it may be dangerous as the greater the angle the wider the spread will become.

Where a combination has a short distance between the fences, if the first fence is jumped to the left and the second to the right, the distance in between the fences may be increased.

The judge's equipment

Officials

The following officials are necessary for all Jumping competitions:

    Judges
    Clerk of the course
    Time-keeper
    Clerk of the scales
    Arena and collecting ring stewards

JUDGES

Every jumping competition is controlled by one or more Judges. In International competitions there are always three and one of these must be from a country which has not been invited to compete at the Show. These Judges are known as the Jury and there is always a senior Judge or President of the Jury in charge.

    Before the competition starts he will:

    Walk the course and satisfy himself that it is fair and suitable for that particular competition.

    Measure and agree the heights and spreads of the obstacles.

    Measure the course and calculate the "Time Allowed" and/or the "Time Limit".

    Check the plan of the course in the collecting ring.

During the competition he will:

Signal the competitor when to start.

Signal the competitor to stop during the round, if necessary, and then signal him to re-start.

Mark the score card for each competitor at each obstacle.

Control the "Time-off" for the re-erection of obstacles when this is permitted.

At the conclusion of each round, total the faults, check the time with the Time-judge and then announce the competitor's score.

If there is a jump-off, check the obstacles for this and then conduct the jump-off in the same way as for the competition.

At the conclusion of the competition he will work out and announce the result.

The following equipment should be available to the Judge:

An electric bell or some means by which he can start and stop competitors.

Two stop-watches.

Score sheets and pencil.

Plan of the course.

Measuring stick.

(Whilst the Judge is responsible for all the above, when the post of Clerk of the Course is filled by an experienced person, the Judge may delegate any or all of the duties in connection with the preparation of the course to him, and will not measure the course himself.)

THE CLERK OF THE COURSE

The Clerk is responsible for planning and erecting the course for each competition.

Before the competition starts he will:

Plan the course.

Erect, measure and set each obstacle.

Measure the length of the course.

Prepare plans of the course and pass one to the Collecting Ring Steward for the information of competitors.

Satisfy himself that he has adequate spare parts in case of damage to obstacles.

Arrange for carpenter with tools to be available.

If the ground is hard, arrange for the landing side of each obstacle to be softened by watering or by putting down peat or sand.

Report to the Judge that the course is ready and correct, and hand him a plan of the course.

During the competition he will:

Supervise the re-erection of any obstacles knocked down.

Ensure that any obstacle touched but not knocked down is checked before the next competitor starts.

Watch the "going" and in wet weather put down sand if it becomes dangerous.

The following equipment should be available to the Clerk of the Course:

Measuring stick.

Measuring tape.

Note book in which particulars of each obstacle are entered so that if it is completely demolished it can be re-erected correctly.

THE TIME-JUDGE

This official is responsible to the Judge for timing each competitor over the course. He may also be required by the Judge to take the "Time-off".

As each competitor finishes his round, the Time-judge will advise the Judge of the exact time taken. If, during a round, a competitor appears likely to exceed the "Time Limit", the Time-judge should first warn the Judge and then notify him of the exact moment when the time is exceeded.

ARENA AND COLLECTING RING STEWARDS

At least one steward will be required in the arena and two in the collecting ring. It is their duty to ensure that the right competitor is ready to jump and enter the ring at the correct time. The Collecting Ring Steward is also responsible for ensuring that the competitors are correctly dressed, and that they are wearing the right number, which he will communicate to the Judge as the competitor enters the arena.

THE CLERK OF THE SCALES

This official is responsible to the Judge that each competitor is "Weighed In" after completing the course. If a competitor fails to make the weight, the Clerk of the Scales must notify the Judge to this effect as quickly as possible.

Classification and Awards

The only faults to be recorded are those incurred during the round. The round will commence when the competitor passes the Starting Line, and finish when he passes the Finishing Line.

The mistakes made by a competitor are recorded either as faults or penalty-seconds, in accordance with the conditions laid down in the programme for the particular competition. Competitions are judged and faults awarded, under F.E.I. Tables A, B or C, or B.S.J.A. Rules Table A or S, as follows:

F.E.I. Table A

(a) *When time is* **not** *a deciding factor*. The awards are decided by totalling the faults incurred during the round. To these are added any penalties for exceeding the "Time Allowed".

In the event of a tie for first place, successive jumps off are compulsory. Other competitors who are equal, but not first, are bracketed together, and share the awards for which they have qualified.

(b) *When time* **is** *stated as a deciding factor*. When two or more competitors are equal, the competitor who has recorded the fastest time will be placed highest. Should there be equality by adding faults incurred over the course with faults incurred for exceeding the "Time Allowed", the competitor with the lowest number of faults incurred over the course will be placed highest.

The scoreboard reads:

MINUTES	AWARDS	CLASS 56	CLEAR ROUNDS
CLASS			481 523 535
1ST No.		COMPETITOR NOW JUMPING 484	568
2ND No.			
3RD No.		LAST COMPETITOR 568 FAULTS 0	
4TH No.			
5TH No.			

F.E.I. Table B and C or B.S.J.A. Table S

The awards are decided by totalling the time taken to complete the course with the penalty-seconds recorded during the round. The competitor with the lowest total is placed highest.

The Jump-off

There will only be a Jump-off for first place. The number of Jumps-off will be stated in the conditions. The Jumps-off must take place over the same course, but the number of obstacles may be reduced in number, and the obstacles raised or enlarged.

Should two or more competitors still be equal at the conclusion of the first Jump-off, these riders will again jump, and successive Jumps-off will take place until a result is obtained.

Under National Rules there will never be more than two Jumps-off, except in a Puissance, and the result will be decided under Tables "A1" to "A4".

Except in the case of a Puissance, the course may never be reduced in the number of obstacles to less than half its original number for the first Jump-off and never less than six obstacles for the first or successive Jumps-off.

If stated in the conditions, time may be used to decide the awards in either the first, second or subsequent Jumps-off.

(NOTE.—In exceptional cases, such as bad light, bad ground conditions, etc., the Judges may permit dividing.)

Rules
(The following pages give an explanation of all the major rules. The faults allotted vary according to the actual competition, and are given on pages 38-39.)

Entering and leaving the arena

When his number is called, a competitor must always enter the arena mounted, and having completed the course must leave the arena mounted unless special permission has been given.

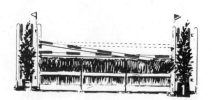

It is a knock-down even if the falling part is stopped in its fall by any other part of the fence

The signal to start will be given by bell, flag or whistle

Starting signal

The signal to start will be given by the bell, whistle or flag, when directed by the judge. This signal will also be used to stop the competitor during a round or to send him out of the arena.

Fences knocked down

An obstacle will be considered to have been knocked down if any portion, including any wing, boundary flag, shrub or other accessory, or a part thereof is lowered, or any part or the whole of it is knocked down, even when the falling part is arrested in its fall or when at least one of its ends is dislodged from its support. But where there are several elements placed one above the other in the same vertical plane; for example when three or more poles are fitted on the same stand, then the dislodgement of the top pole only is penalised. Should the bottom rail or part fall, there will be no penalty.

If a fence is composed of several parts to be taken in one jump by the horse, extra faults will not be incurred even if more than one part or the whole fence is knocked down.

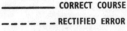

CORRECT COURSE
RECTIFIED ERROR

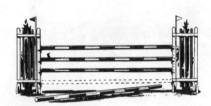

Where all the parts of a fence are in the same vertical plane the dislodgment of the top part only will be penalised. The dislodgment shown above incurs no faults

The following are defined as **Disobediences** and will be penalised as such:

(a) Rectified error or deviation of the course

There is an error of the course if the rider does not follow the course as on the plan, disregards any of the compulsory turning flags, or misses a fence. To rectify an error of the course the rider must, before jumping another fence, return to the correct course.

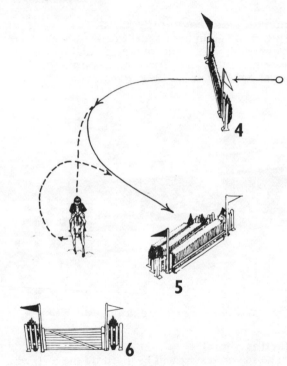

Rectified error of course

(b) Refusal

A horse is said to have refused if he stops in front of a fence. Stopping in front of a fence, without knocking it down and without reining back, followed immediately by a standing jump, is not a refusal.

If the halt is sustained, or if the horse reins back even a single pace, a refusal has taken place.

Should the horse, in refusing, knock down a fence, the clock will be stopped at once. If the disobedience is at a single obstacle or the first part of a multiple obstacle, 6 seconds will be added to the total time taken. If at the second part of a multiple obstacle or at the third or further part, 8 or 10 seconds respectively will be added. If horse and/or rider fall, the clock will not be stopped until the Rider has re-mounted.

If a competitor knocks down one part of a multiple obstacle and then refuses or runs out at the next part without knocking it down, the clock is stopped as for a knockdown resulting from a disobedience. The penalties of 8 or 10 seconds are applied according to whether the disobedience occurs at the second, third or subsequent parts of a multiple obstacle.

If a horse, having knocked down a fence in refusing, jumps the fence before it is re-erected, he is eliminated.

The fall. If the shoulders and quarters have touched the ground, it is a fall

A nervous moment, but no penalty

Disobédiences (continued)

(c) Run-out

A horse is said to have run-out should he, not being under proper control, avoid the obstacle which should have been jumped.

If the horse jumps a fence outside the flags marking its extremities it will be considered a run-out.

Having run-out the horse must return and jump the fence, should he not do so he will be eliminated.

(d) Resistance

It is considered a resistance, if the horse, wherever he may be, refuses to go forward, stops, naps, reins back or turns round, etc.

(e) Knocking down a flag which marks a compulsory turning point is not penalised.

(f) Circling during any part of the course, except to retake the track after a refusal or run-out.

Fall

(a) *Fall of rider*. A rider is considered to have fallen when he is separated from his horse, which has not fallen, so that he has to remount.

(b) *Fall of horse*. A horse is considered to have fallen when the shoulders and quarters have touched either the ground or the obstacle and the ground.

Should a loose horse jump a fence or pass through the finish, it will not be penalised.

A riderless horse will not be penalised for any occurrence whilst unmounted, such as jumping a fence or passing the finish

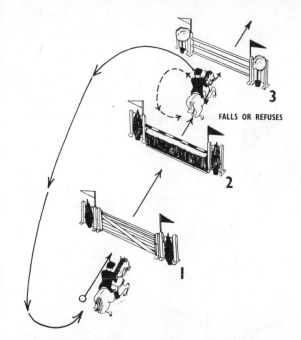

The rider must retake the course at the first part of the combination. Failure means elimination

FAULTS AT COMBINATIONS

Clearing an obstacle which is a double or treble constitutes a particular test, and the fences cannot

therefore be separated. Consequently should a horse refuse, run out, or fall between any of these fences, the rider must re-start at the first fence of the combination. Faults at each single fence of the combination are totalled.

Knocking over the boundary flag penalised 4 faults

FLAGS

Flags are used to mark the limits of a fence, and the fence must be jumped between these flags. A red flag will always be used on the right, a white one on the left.

These flags must be independent of the stands or wings of the fence.

If the flag is knocked down when the fence is knocked down, no additional penalty is incurred

WEIGHT

(a)   At International Shows the minimum weight to be carried by all competitors is 74.8 k, but

Unauthorised assistance

Unauthorised assistance during a round is forbidden. The decision as to what is unauthorised assistance is the responsibility of the Judges. Bringing back a loose horse after a fall, or helping the rider to re-adjust saddlery, or to remount, is not considered unauthorised assistance.

Accidents

(a) A competitor who is injured after the commencement of his round cannot be replaced.
(b) An injured horse cannot be replaced.

Saddlery

The saddlery is optional, but all manner of blinkers are prohibited under International Rules.

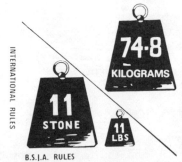

(b) **In the B.S.J.A.** National Championship the B.S.J.A. Olympic Trial and the Leading Show Jumper of the Year Championship a minimum weight of 74.8 k must be carried by all competitors.

SPEEDS

(a) Under F.E.I. Rules the minimum speeds are:

Ordinary jumping competitions—
350m (382 yds.) per minute

Test competitions—
300m (327 yds.) per minute

Nation's Cup competitions—
400m (436 yds.) per minute

(b) *Under B.S.J.A. Rules.*
Ordinary jumping competitions—
275m (300 yds.) per minute.

TIME ALLOWED

The "Time Allowed" is the time within which the competitor must complete the course to avoid being penalised. The "Time Allowed" is calculated on the speed and the length of the course.

TIME LIMIT

The "Time Limit" is double the "Time Allowed", and exceeding this entails elimination.

Faults and Time Penalties

F.E.I. "Table A" and B.S.J.A.

1st Disobedience	..	..	3 faults
2nd Disobedience	..	..	6 faults
3rd Disobedience	..	..	Elimination

(Faults for disobedience are cumulative, not only at the same fence, but throughout the same round.)

Fence knocked down	..	..	4 faults
One or more feet in the water	..	4 faults

(Landing on the marking tape is penalised as for in the water.)

Fall of horse or rider or both   ..   8 faults

(The faults for the fall are additional to any other faults incurred at the same time.)

Exceeding the "Time Allowed" $\frac{1}{4}$ fault for every second.

One or more feet in the water—4 faults.

Landing on the tape is penalised as in the water.

F.E.I. "Table B"

Fence knocked down .. .. 10 penalty seconds

One or more feet in the water.. 10 penalty seconds

Third disobedience .. .. Elimination

(Falls and the first two disobediences are penalised automatically by the extra time taken.)

F.E.I. "Table C"

Fence knocked down   Appropriate penalty seconds, see Table C

One or more feet in the water..   as above

Third disobedience .. .. Elimination

(Falls and the first two disobediences are penalised automatically by the extra time taken.)

Table C

TABLE OF PENALTIES IN SECONDS FOR EACH FAULT OVER OBSTACLES

Metres	Number of Jumps or attempts															
	23	22	21	20	19	18	17	16	15	14	13	12	11	10	9	8
200	—	—	—	—	—	—	—	—	—	—	—	3	3	3	4	4
300	—	—	—	—	—	—	—	—	—	3	4	5	5	5	5	6
400	—	—	—	—	—	—	—	4	4	5	5	6	7	7	8	8
500	—	—	—	—	—	5	5	5	5	6	7	7	7	8	8	—
600	—	—	—	5	5	5	6	6	7	7	8	9	9	10	10	—
700	—	5	5	6	6	6	7	7	7	8	9	9	10	11	11	—
800	5	6	6	6	7	7	7	8	8	9	9	10	11	12	—	—
900	6	6	7	7	7	7	8	9	9	10	11	11	12	13	—	—
1000	7	7	7	7	8	8	9	9	10	11	11	12	13	15	—	—

Under all Rules the following will always incur elimination:

(a) Failing to be ready to enter the arena when called.

(b) Jumping any fence in the ring before starting the course.

(c) Showing any fence to the horse before starting, or after a refusal.

(d) Crossing the starting line before the starting signal is given.

(e) Failing to cross the starting line within sixty seconds of the starting signal.

(f) Entering or leaving the arena dismounted without special permission.

(g) Resistance of the horse during the round at any one time exceeding sixty seconds.

(h) Jumping a fence without having rectified an error of the course.

(i) Jumping a fence not forming part of the course.

(j) Passing the wrong side of a boundary flag if not rectified.

(k) Exceeding the time limit.

(l) Jumping a fence which has been knocked down before it has been re-set, and without waiting for the signal to re-start.

(m) After a disobedience or fall at a combination, failing to re-start jumping over the whole combination.

(n) Failing to cross the finishing line mounted before leaving the arena.

(o) The horse or rider leaving the arena, mounted or loose, before completion of the round.

(p) Receiving unauthorised assistance whether solicited or not.

(q) Failing to have the required minimum weight when weighing in after completion of the round.

(r) Knocking down the automatic timing equipment.

(s) A 3rd disobedience during a round.

Special Competitions

ACCUMULATOR COMPETITION

In this competition there will be from five to seven fences of progressive size and difficulty. Points are allotted as follows:

No. 1 Obstacle cleared ..	..	1 point
No. 2 Obstacle cleared ..	..	2 points
and so on to No. 7 Obstacle cleared ..	..	7 points

Maximum points 15, 21 or 28 according to the number of obstacles. Refusals, disobedience, etc., are penalised by the usual penalties.

The competitor with the highest score in points after deduction of any penalty points, including those for being over the time allowed, will be the winner. In the event of equality for first place there will be one jump-off in which time will decide.

HAVE A GAMBLE STAKES

This is a timed Competition and takes place over a course of from 12 to 14 obstacles, each carrying a number of points, points are relative to the difficulty of the obstacle.

Six obstacles are valued at 100, 90, 80, 70, 60 and 50 points, and of the remainder, two are valued at 40, two at 30, two at 20 and two at 10 points. If an obstacle is knocked down a Competitor may not jump or attempt to jump it again.

The Competitor having passed through the start will jump the obstacle designated as the first obstacle, thereafter the Competitor may jump any obstacle in either direction and any order within a time limit of 60 seconds. No obstacle may be jumped more than twice.

Should a Competitor attempt to jump an obstacle and refuse he must continue to endeavour to jump that obstacle from the same direction, and may not proceed to another one until the obstacle first attempted has been jumped.

The bell will be rung at the conclusion of 60 seconds. An obstacle will not be considered as having been jumped and points will not be scored until the horse's fore legs touch the ground on landing.

The Competitor with the highest score in points will be the winner.

MULTIPLE GAMBLERS STAKES

The fences for this competition will be of varying heights and difficulty, and a large playing card will be placed by each fence to indicate its value, large obstacles being of greater value than smaller ones, i.e. Ace 14 points, King 13 points, Queen 12 points, Knave 11 points, and so on.

The competitor must jump seven obstacles only of his choice within a time limit of two minutes. They may be jumped in any order and from either direction, and any obstacle may be jumped as many times as the competitor wishes, but once that obstacle has been knocked down it may not be jumped again. If a competitor jumps or attempts to jump more than seven obstacles he will be eliminated. Once a competitor attempts to jump an obstacle he must continue to attempt to jump it from the same direction and may not proceed to another one until he has succeeded. Each obstacle jumped clear will be awarded the points indicated by the playing cards. No points are awarded for a fence knocked down. The winner will be the competitor who obtains the most number of points, and in the event of equality, time will decide.

TAKE YOUR OWN LINE COMPETITION

In this competition competitors are allowed to select the order in which they jump the course of obstacles which have been built for the competition. Each fence must only be jumped once, but can be jumped from either direction. The winner is the one who jumps the complete course in the fastest time and with fewest faults. This competition is judged under Table S (Speed).

Printed in Great Britain by John Blackburn Ltd. Leeds.